KT-462-019

THE GREY AMONG THE GREEN

THE GREY
AMONG THE GREEN
John Fuller

Chatto & Windus LONDON

Published in 1988 by
Chatto & Windus Ltd
30 Bedford Square
London WC1B 3RP

A CIP Catalogue record for this book is available from the British Library

ISBN 0 7011 3333 3

Acknowledgements are due to the following, in which some of these
poems first appeared: *Carte d'Europa, Isis, Oxford Poetry, Poems for
Shakespeare, Poetry Book Society Anthology, Poetry Book Society
Supplement, Poetry Review, Poetry Australia, Poetry* (Chicago),
*Sotheby's International Poetry Competition 1982 Anthology, The Times
Literary Supplement.*

Copyright © John Fuller 1988

Photoset by
Rowland Phototypesetting Ltd
Bury St Edmunds, Suffolk

Printed in Great Britain by
Redwood Burn Ltd
Trowbridge, Wiltshire

Contents

THE GREY AMONG THE GREEN

Breakfast

Mornings restore us to the physical
With the clink of familiar slight purpose,
Toying with a log-jam of All Bran
In milk almost blue, like a wrist.

The spoon has the weight and arched curve
Of a torso prepared for pleasure or pain,
Reminding us of dreams where we hunted
Free spirits down infinite spaces.

But the bowl, though endless, is finite,
A perfect white circle, with deceitful flowers,
A shape matched by the defining zones
Of our weakest spots: collar, belt.

Dead Clothes

Dead clothes tell us what we have outlasted,
Weird surfaces of the self, less hardy
Though more prominent, projections and transmissions
To a world that requires sartorial mnemonics,
Since nudity is the one disguise that discreates our Selves.

I have worn some ridiculous clothes in my time,
Not least in boyhood, to say nothing of later years:
Leggings with buttons done up with a button-hook;
A grey beret with a stalk; a ginger suit
In which I was especially roguish
Behind a hot-plate in a hotel ballroom
At an annual party for the Deaf-and-Dumb;
Separate collars, with a stud to bruise the throat;
A long green overcoat, done up at the neck.

What went on inside clothes like these has been mostly
    lost,
And my memory of the clothes will not last for ever.

Blow Up

That colourless unmoving world again!
The old contact pushing at its edges,
Not only the strain of sphere to contain square

But the unaccustomed size, re-creating
A periphery like absolute annihilation,
A new reminder of the fatal limits of vision.

The unconsidered detail proves to be part
Of the design: beyond an arm, beneath a chin,
Things appear to be about to happen.

Were we there? Did we once know? Was
It *our* one eye that squeezed its flat world
Into the random history of a paper wallet?

Or maybe that is us, after all, in the picture,
Unrecognisable. We were all young once,
Strange faces, the dead light from stars.

The Art of Forgetting

Swivelling from a damp duvet at an hour
Too late for sleep, too early for work,
I wonder if sleep and its rapt drenchings
Are part of the art of forgetting or remembering.

Since whatever grips the mind in these dark hours
Is distinct, pungent, but elusive as smoke.
In the morning it is there and it is not there.
Who knows what it meant or what it means?

Writing this, it occurs to me to recall
A prep-room thirty years ago: Lister, owlish
At chess, scornful of fooling; Campling cutting card
For trains; brown Ryback laughing, tamping a rocket.

All is gone, the room, the house itself gone,
To allow for a widened road easing the traffic
Into and out of the seething heart of dreams.
Forgetting? Remembering? It seems to be all the same.

Equation

A perfect ease of conversation!
I have never managed it so well!
    The eyes sparkle, appraising
Other eyes, like an equation.
    The answer is amazing!
Where will it lead? Who can tell?

And then there is the insistent question
Of what the images can mean
    That come at times like these
With their perfectly decent suggestion
    Of impossibilities,
Wonderful things that have never been.

There's never time for a decision.
Life is made of sterner stuff!
    So, friends, dismiss the thought
That this is a constructive vision:
    As always, as we've been taught,
Life itself is quite enough.

And so goodbye: we'll save for later
The moment when these things are faced.
    Goodbye, dear friends, goodbye!
Goodbye to life itself, creator
    Of that self-serving lie
That life is good enough to waste.

Bud

Mildest of winters keeps the heart
Stirred once again to make a start
   On the old things.
A file of letters like a trap
Gapes. The mind draws on its sap
   For some new rings.

The slumber of the wasps is ours,
Dying in carton, far from flowers,
   Or so we reason.
But now the sun shines through a tree
Across my desk, enticingly,
   Out of its season

As though the year forgot its drift,
Discovering within its gift
   A strange remission
From cycles of that long disease
Which every estimate agrees
   Is our condition.

And so I stretch and seek the air
In the dead garden, finding there
   Something like you:
One paler and intense ellipse
Signals a bud among the hips,
   And one will do.

To Each Other

Not the calm centre that you think me,
 Not quite there,
Perhaps quietly struggling to be different,
 To be elsewhere
In some sense that you would find absurd
 Or vaguely resent
As being not, when you wish me moved,
 Quite what you meant.

Well, who cares? Life drains away
 Despite the weight
Of hands, eyes, custom, design,
 And it is late
To establish reasons for preferring
 The things we prefer
When now it seems grotesque to imagine
 That they might occur.

Light

Flat looks, flat smiles, dead things:
Ordinary purposes
We follow like a smell
To root, to snuffle up.

But all the time there is
This light, oblique, refracted,
Falling on this and that,
Falling as if by chance.

This light translates the world
Until it does not matter
When and where and how
The final darkness comes.

The light is compelled to gather
Like tears in a ghost's eye
In a long desperation,
And the ghost is you, is only you.

Disappointments

All over the city they are waiting for the night
Like a courtroom hoping for a popular verdict:
The longer it seems, the less likely the pleasure.

Or rather, the pleasure belongs to that whim of authority
Which insists upon the pronouncing of a prearranged
    sentence
And forbids all freedom of association.

Who *is* that spoilsport, querulous, ancient, severe,
Writing down the fatal words in his book?
It is our condition, first and last judge, who condemns.

At the centres of passion they queue without protesting.
Attendance is frequent in the offices of desire,
But interviews granted are few. The post is unfilled.

When disappointments feed upon themselves
Who dares to say that the diet is quite unsuitable
For the strapping lads they might become if they chose?

Must our delights, then, fall like fruit from a tree
That impatience shakes with the hand of fulfilment?
Shall we grow to relish the small, the stunted, the bitter?

Longing

Have you, too, been aware
Of a sort of something inside you,
Something uncertainly there
Like something you never tried?

And its claims are not defunct
Like hopes that age has cancelled,
That the passing of time has junked,
Like many old hopes and plans.

It isn't really dead:
It stirs like a slow April,
It gathers to a head,
It takes some sort of shape.

It's like a faculty
Unused, an eye in hiding
That senses it can see.
That comes to life inside.

Through all the ridiculous hours
It angles for attention
Like the clamour of spring flowers
And their innocent stench.

What is it that we most miss?
What do we have and have not?
In the last analysis
It's what we need to have.

And can we create what we miss?
Merely the fact that we sense it,
Merely my writing this
Is a kind of consequence.

And from these words there flows
A surge of strange fulfilment
Without its object. That goes
Outwards, and where it will.

Gone

Gone, gone, all gone,
Blown, and the gloom is towering:
Remains the dull, the civil,
The patient, the put-upon,
The chill roots that shrivel
After the first flowering.

Now for the decline.
Beauty speeds away
From the seed of our creating,
Following the line
Of its own accelerating,
The simple growth of play.

Often there is this sense
Of being beaten flat
In order to make the past
A kind of recompense.
Some things that we outlast
Were worth much more than that.

Wednesday

Wednesday, black rabbit, seven years old,
You were silent all your short life as though
   Entrusted with a secret
   You could not be sure of keeping.

Easily startled, you would never turn your head
But stared in a still alarm through creepered brick
   Into that missing meadow
   Where danger would be a delight.

Not the eyes, a cloudy lidless brown,
But scissored ears positioned like microphones
   Brought the imaginary
   Misty horizons near.

Sometimes you dashed in joy from bed to bed
Like a comedian with surprises in the wings,
   Feet avoiding the fronds
   With a fastidious flick.

Not so many abortive burrows were yours
But the same one, not serious, under the rose.
   Your preferred occupations
   Were transporting paper

Or making circles around our wary heels
When on dewy evenings we trod
   With purpose or excuse
   Into your green domain.

Sturdy little president of the lawn!
We ignored your private moods; your gaiety
   Was at most a flourish
   In our casual moments.

And when you were found, a stretched effigy,
A hard object so much like yourself
   But weirdly without motion
   And feared like an impostor,

The ensuing sorrow was the strangest thing,
A conscious grieving in a larger happiness
   That seemed designed to absorb
   Its choking negative.

Whatever strange lessons of death we learned
Touching your flat still body or pushing turf
   Into impromptu place
   Above the disturbed earth,

We prefer to make of you a remembered image
That accords with our myth of perpetual contentment,
   Of life as an unfolding
   Towards an unseen horizon.

And now at evening in the summer air,
With wine and fruit unfinished on the table,
   The candle sculpts a soft
   But meagre circle of shadows.

And as night comes, the garden is suddenly empty
Of a black shape in the blackness, coming from nowhere,
   Coming at an idle call
   Though never making a sound.

Suppose

Suppose your future is to be
Too little and too briefly loved,
 Though not by me.

Suppose that you discover how
The things you most regret are those
 About you now

That seem so easily achieved,
So lightly kept, and over which
 You will have grieved

Thinking that they would last and last
As now the present seems the perfect
 Gift of the past

And tells of feelings handed on
Like sounds in consort, link by link,
 Till they are gone.

Suppose all this: would knowing where
And when the change occurred do much
 To make you care?

Hardly, for you'll remember such
A wealth of missing things it will
 Not matter much

And even if a day brings pain
It will be gladly worn in its
 Unbroken chain

And grieving is a joy, my dear,
That you will sadly soon discover,
 As I do here.

Daughter

Once inside my head
The thought is hard to get out:
    Another daughter.

You were never ours.
Photographs showed you missing
    And no one noticed.

Intention was blind:
How near was your conception
    We shall never know.

The disqualified
Candidates can't believe the
    Office is unfilled.

You don't exist, but
Nobody can take your place:
    That space has been booked.

Three faces suggest
The fourth: compass points of the
    Parental axes.

Words like little loves
Presiding over a map
    For future journeys.

Prospero's secret
Sadness: I had peopled else
    This isle with daughters.

Only the subject
Of unuseful poetry:
    What never occurred.

Lawn Games

The rose shoots again
On its dead stump: there are things
    Not to be thought of.

Rambling blue flowers
Fade on the stone: bottle and glass
    Exchange their inches.

A heel on one knee,
A slight air cooling the sleeve:
    The eyes are restless.

Each grass blade aims high,
Each green corner joins arms with
    Its neighbour: a lawn.

Hoops turn the lawn to
A lucky six: the sun looks
    Down on a red ball.

Palace of pleasures:
Beauty is ignorant of
    Being imagined.

Five doves on the lawn:
Celestial fingerprint,
    A kiss from earth's lips.

Nape, elbow, instep:
Her rug settles after a
    Smooth flight from Turkey.

Ten toes, heels lifted:
Ankle bones like buds of wings,
    Eyes shut to the sky.

Names and Faces

Late afternoon sounds:
The laughter of friends,
The filling of water
And kettle-lid's clatter
Heard across rooms
That forget their names
Like rooms that are haunted
Until they are entered
With tea and talk,
At which they wake
To lamps switched
And trays fetched
With steaming cups,
Cake, and perhaps
New contact prints
Of faces like saints
Staring in surprise
(Or smiles, or unease)
Over and over
At one-eyed lover —
Matter for grimace
Of pride, of course,
And tall tales
Of broken rules,
Of friends charmed
And things performed:
Another bundle
Of camera scandal.
Evening extends
Like desert sands,
Darkness comes up
At every sip,
And now the room's
Alive with names

Like an oasis,
With names and faces
In a lit space.

Emily's Chopin

Beyond the bedroom wall
Through which a knocked goodnight
Sounds like the cheerful call
Of an escapologist
To his charmed audience
Who only dimly sense
That once out of their sight
Already from his wrist
The playful shackles fall,

Beyond that boundary
Where brilliant high-fee'd sleep
Is willing to act for free
Who here takes nightly bribes
For cases that he bungles,
Her dreams are thick as jungles,
Precipitous and deep
As falls, down which lost tribes
Row chanting to the sea.

But first upon the air
Drift the pale thunderings
From muted record-player
Of Chopin in a tragic
Elevated mood.
Melodies, we conclude,
Are yearning wraith-like things
That offer prescriptive magic
The sleepless gladly share.

Lucy's Daffodil

Poorly finger, it didn't know
What it was doing. Now cut in water
It preaches from the tumbril of spring
A last speech on survival. It leans
Into a mysterious angle of beckoning
As if for inspection or attention,
Turning all sound green.

Chill flower, its ribbon pumped
With air, one jewel on the stem
Like a lost bathysphere,
It reaches from the rattling window as if
Hammered from what little light
Winter has admitted, scared
To be reclaimed by the wind.

Tissue lifts from the stalk knuckle.
The baby bell is haunted, nowhere
Else to turn. Its silent yell
Is like a gasp for oxygen
Claiming the whole room in the name
Of an emotion still to be invented.
What does the sun say? I can't hear.

Avoid Contact with the Eyes

You are safe here, in a protective envelope
That stays the shape of your body, warmer than blood,
A horizontal cubicle with a levitated
Door of water, a flooded sarcophagus
To revive in, anointed. If you cut the cord
The life will leak away again. If you sing
Someone will rush in, pretending alarm,
To see for one steamy moment two big eyes
And meringue hair. He will rush out again
For fear of being involved in your inviolable
Voyage and its exciting but innocent islands,
For though in that amused instant you lie
As still as art or geology, there on the edge
He will see the dangerous potion in sudden close-up
And the instructions are quite clear on the bottle.

Synopsis for a German Novella

The Doctor is glimpsed among his mulberry trees.
The dark fruits disfigure the sward like contusions.
He is at once aloof, timid, intolerant
Of all banalities of village life,
And yet is stupefied by loneliness.

Continually he dreams of the company he craves for,
But he challenges it and bores it to tears whenever
It swims uncertainly into his narrow orbit.
Meetings, however relished in their prospect,
Seem only to be arrangements for departures.

Exemplum: the spruce Captain and his vampire wife
With her token fur hat and veil, like a bandage
Extemporised by a bat. It seems that exercise
Keeps the Captain's horse in a permanent lather.
The wife suffers from a disabling ennui.

What more likely than a harmless liaison?
At their first meeting the scenario is as obvious
As a cheese. Her eyes, half-lidded, turn away,
The cup lifted to her lips. The Captain has questions
About the flooding of the water-meadow.

A furious but undirected energy governs her soul,
Listless as she seems on the surface. It is
A libido on auto-destruct. Opportunities
Occur, but the Doctor, in complacent rectitude,
Bows himself off the stage of further meetings.

He devotes himself to his patients. They, however,
Begin to avoid him as if he has some dreadful disease.
When the Captain is lost on the glacier, his horse
Riderless, returning to graze on the bowling-green,
The Doctor is suspected. It is most unfair.

Meanwhile, his orphaned cousins go ahead
With their threatened law-suit. At first he is amused.
He meets their legal representative over
A schnapps in the Bahnhof Buffet, and is compromised
By the leather luggage of the absconding wife.

He claims to have found a cure for the epidemic of goitres
But only succeeds in killing two maids and a barley farmer.
The Captain's wife is staying at Interlaken
With the Schoolmaster's wastrel son. Her insane letters
Are read out in court, evidence of the Doctor's malpractice.

Only his good old Nurse refuses to disbelieve him.
On her death-bed she grips his fingers tightly
And mutters inaudibly about the lost diaries.
There is nothing now to prevent the red-haired cousins
From taking complete control of his estate.

The Doctor has lost everything and gained nothing.
At the back of his mind there is still the slight hope
That time will explain to him his crucial role.
He becomes a cutter of peat, and realises
That it is never quite easy enough to disappear.

The Curable Romantic

1

Returning from the encounter
He finds the room excited:
Walls flash mirrors like glances

That require the intended meeting of eyes,
And furniture is eager to be married
To the restless shapes it was made for.

Chess pieces go off quietly like pistols
In the irregular rhythm of a *paso doble*.
Lamps blaze, and books somnambulate.

One of these, settling in his hand like another hand,
Tells him insistently of a reckless love
And closes shyly with a sigh.

When he puts it back on the shelf
The room subsides at last into calm
And he is left alone with his remembrances.

She is in them still, but smaller.
The eyes close in weariness and containment.
The room waits for her.

2

The curable romantic has written five letters
In three days. He knows he will get answers
To none of them, because he has not sent them.
And because it is in the lines between the lines
That everything to be spoken remains unspoken.

3

Let him, like the classic poets, take
An eyebrow here, an opinion there
To assemble his dear impossible.

That way of pausing, this of smiling,
One habit of turning the chin to the shoulder,
Another of looking up from a book in surprise.

No doubt there are more intimate features,
The blind creases that open in the dark,
Nipple, wrist, nape and tongue.

All the relaxed and extended surfaces!
The stretched skin and hair of dreams!
At such times the features are blurred.

He must abandon these choice catalogues
And maintain his friendly relationship
With the actual, the possible, the ordinary.

For it is here, after all, isn't it,
That the ideal features derive? Here is
Imperfection, the truly loveable.

4
The curable romantic is lying in his bath
Having displaced the customary volume.
He is stripped of all his illusions except one:
That this finally which he is lumbered with
Is too solid to be anything but a permanent burden.

5
But then, it is simply waste and rehearsal.
The conversation leads nowhere, drifting
Short of the evening.

Groomed for companionship, the practised faces
Speak against the drawing of the curtains
With fatal fervour.

Doors open and close, and the rooms
Are emptier. He finishes a half-inch
Not his own.

Is it, he wonders, at all different elsewhere?
Above the roofscape a restless flock of birds
Gives no answer.

6

So we know that the hand
Reaches half in confidence
Half in timidity
For its due happiness.

There is a respect for souls
Who seem to share the quest,
A glee with them, and yet
Perhaps no ultimate trust.

Suppose, then, a silence
Not damaged but rueful,
The hand reaching out,
Not grasping, not retreating.

Maybe this is also
Your quiet satisfaction?
A face flowers in beauty,
In absorbed isolation.

7

Looking again on this face
He abandons all resolutions.

Reassumes the illusions
That yesterday he resigned

As he pedalled vigorously,
Hunched at a snail's pace

Towards the dead familiar
Landscape of his life

As he certainly will again
Tonight, and every night.

8
The curable romantic has thoughts of becoming pure
   spirit:
He waves all clocks away and scribbles incessantly.
His meals are still-lives and he smiles as he talks.
What good is it to say to him: 'Tomorrow you will be
   hungry.
Tomorrow you will sit down to the feast of your own
   heart?'

Eloge des Gammes

You think you've come far enough for better answers.
For the bitten thumb, the shirt riding over the hip,
And dancing in up five steps at one bound

When the sun first goes behind the trees
And the host is opening bottles. For a hand
On the arm, the fingers splayed like a difficult chord.

For the conspirator's laugh, saying: 'Wait. No, really,
Wait there in the hall. I've something to show you.
You won't believe it!' For the visit already begun

At the hour of committees which is intriguingly
Advanced by the time you arrive. For the square letter
Which came after you left and is still there.

For the glance from parted hair thrown towelled and damp
Behind the ears, and a cigarette put out
Which is still smouldering, you notice, the next day.

But of course (of course!) you will find that there is still
Much travelling to be done. The indefinable
Eludes the contained excitement of its seeking

As from an upstairs room the scales ascend
Farther and farther, regular, luminous, distinct,
And every note is perfect, and still more perfect.

Incident

Love is a railway terminal.
The train can't start until it's full.
I saw you on the platform there
But I didn't have the fare.
Life is very dull.
Couldn't you have let me know?

Love is the demon crossword setter.
Love is the blank, the missing letter.
Love is the word inside my head
I somehow never said.
No one to kiss me better.
Couldn't you have let me know?

Love is an empty telephone.
No change. Only the dialling tone.
Love is the waiting, and the rage
At finding you engaged.
And now I'm on my own.
Couldn't you have let me know?

Love is an incident at Newry.
Love is the verdict of the jury.
Love is the feeling that I saved
To help me to be brave.
It's my guilt. It's my fury.
Couldn't you have let me know?

Space Invader

Each little thing is arranged. The hotel key,
Numbered like a convict with its ball and chain,
Is slipped inside a folded *Sunday Times*.

The prisoner is allowed one telephone call:
An insistent ostinato devours his money
As plausible devices are capably launched.

Fidel is polishing glasses with the motion
He used for grinding pepper on her squid.
You time him as he turns back to the shelves.

You miss the unread paper and wonder about
The DLY NIGHT O under her arm. It takes
Four minutes to appear to enjoy a strega.

Fidel stares and yawns, a silent Wotan.
It's eleven all the way up the creaking stairs,
A crude conspiracy of brass and carpet.

The rooms are meaningless as an index entry
To a name you forget even as you look it up
Because you are tired or know the search is useless.

She is already waiting, a lump in the bed
You do not know which side to get into.
The light switches are conjuror's apparatus.

And now the program begins. It is a version
Of the familiar, with an alien object. A makeshift,
Though with arcade features. Worth every penny.

Voyage

From meeting on pavements
With raffia weals from the shopping
And a grin for news

To lips on places
Formerly merely admired
And nothing spoken

Is to wake on board,
To slip below the horizon,
To steer by stars.

Who knows what happened
That fateful night in harbour?
A complete blank!

One thing is certain:
There's miles to travel yet
And no going back.

Little Mouths, Little Ghosts

Mouths make shapes like ghosts
That do not know if they
Are space or skin or

Something between surprise
And hope and restlessness,
That nomad harvest of

Fine hairs, exhalations
From the blood, the lips'
Sebaceous pasture where

Orations of protest
Are starved of the air
That could deliver them,

The throat locked between
Urgency and denial
Like the engaged tone,

Alive with pleasure
At the perfect pressure
(5 lbs per square inch) which

Launches these ambassadors
Of the spirit, these spooks
Of the tongue, themselves

Haunted by time that will
Uncreate them, and by silence,
And the nearness of a face.

Eyes and Lips

Reading the lesson of the eyes
And paragraphs of lips,
Hands need only touch the face
As if to keep their place

And eyes have nothing at all to do
But speak to other eyes,
And lips absorb their own reflection
Without objection.

Eyes move guiltily, uncertain
Of their coordinates.
Lips receive distinct impressions
In lengthy sessions.

These faculties communicate
With freely borrowed roles
When the whole skin surface goes walking,
Good looking, small talking.

But then, as if such paradoxes
Were not enough, consider:
All this was simply what eyes did.
This was what lips said.

A Surprise

All day the window squared off sky
With half a bare ash tree in it,
Grey clouds inching across shut glass
In a wind that made outside sounds,
Nosing slate and cold stone as though
Our mysterious shelter drew
An inquisitive animal
Back again to its frustration.

All afternoon we construed our
Books as cracking logs shifted in
The black grate like restless sleepers,
Never looking up as time slowed,
Till suddenly we sensed the wind
Had dropped and there at the undrawn
Curtains to surprise us was clear
Dusk. And Hesperus, like an eye.

The Visitor

How can I begin?
And who will let me in?
I lean upon the far side of your mind
As if a door could learn
It had a hinge to turn
And, opening, disclose what was behind.
I whisper the appealing word
You claim you do not wish to hear, but surely heard.

Windows, as windows must,
Yawn on their jaws of rust.
Their catches snap, their webs are stretched and broken.
Curtains on their wings
Stretch like the folded wings
Of some dark-lidded bird too soon awoken,
For whom a gently sleeping wood
Makes restless sounds that it would fathom if it could.

And now a little air
Stirs in the rafters where
Tied sprays of leaves and herbs are slowly turning.
It wakes the drowsy fire
And makes the flames leap higher
To tell the silent room that they are burning.
It corners rugs with its embrace
As though by folding down a page to mark its place.

You find me in the gloom
Of the chill morning room
Before the fire is stirred or curtains drawn,
And through the ticking day
As hours slip away
I shadow small things struggling to be born.
I am the chimney and the mouse
And all the little noises of the midnight house.

The cat before the coals
From which the smoke in scrolls
Describes the movements of the massy air
Knows that I'm inside
And have a place to hide,
Although her blinking will not tell her where
And motionless her paws lie curled
About the dreaming suburbs of her tabby world.

On and about I go,
Carefully to and fro,
To keep the bedclothes you threw back in tangles.
Silently I explore
Your papers on the floor,
Arrange the furniture at curious angles
In rooms to which you are returning
To find a pan still simmering or lamp still burning.

And now you are aware
That I am living where
You notice these familiar surfaces,
And though I am unseen
You know where I have been
And understand what secret motive is
By now implicit in that being,
Impelling you to this necessity of seeing.

I am the secret print
Of fire within the flint.
I am the sleeping spark that dreams of tinder.
I am the wood that sings.
I am the tongue that springs
To sudden life upon the dying cinder.
I am the burning in your eye
That sets the world alight and will not let it die.

Swimming at Night

Swimmers intend to be born again. Their laughter
And purpose bespeak a creature of consciousness

Even when descending a mad path to the night sea,
Stumbling at a damp curtain of black air

When the blackness itself has secret shades of black:
Purse black, space black, the black over the shoulder.

The eye that has no need to see looks nowhere,
But hands reach out for the bond of touch

Whose intention is some sort of commitment to the
    elements,
Linked and cautious on the delirious gradient,

Elements which perform their nuptials like a great drama
Proving an expressive bond of contraries:

Clouds heavy with the charge of a ready storm
Bounce their energy from the fused ceiling of air.

Thunder in a flickering jumble of light in the hills
Exposes the sea's swirling danger and glamour

And the damp is distinguished as an insistent fine rain
That joins sky and tide in drifts of forgetting.

This is a ritual where nothing was known beforehand,
Urged by the meteorological preamble.

Pleasures must be insignificant beside the attention
Of like to like, salt blood, salt water.

Clothes are bundled from the drizzle, a stub
Of candle flickering in the dredged hulk,

A dead boat beached in the invisible sand
That dwindles, though groined and lantern-steady,

Tiny along the shore as blackness reassumes
The crawling skin like a vestment.

And now hands break the sea as thunder breaks again,
And diving shocks the depths to a response:

Turbid with lit plankton like spokes and clocks,
The salt galaxies are bruised into being by our bodies.

Little fitful beacons of dull watery light
Sharpening the dark as the gallons glop about us

And the air splits and cracks and the rain falls
Alive on the blind surface of the sea.

It was not what we intended. It is not us.
It is something quite other. It is the first thing.

This strange submarine light is a hoarded scattering
Like the earliest seeds, like the touch of kisses.

It is damaged stars, like blotted lightning,
Like points to be joined that would give us wings.

Being born is a gasping and drenching.
It is cold and clean as the dead centre of night.

We have no thought of returning,
Consciousness switched off at the source.

Reckless of gravity, the candle lost,
We strike in light and darkness from the shore.

The Cry

You heard that noise in Louis's wood?
Was it the creature that he heard
Three times one night and was afraid
To go much further than the gate
Because it was so late?

The pines that took his life to stretch
Above the skyline try to touch
The sea-westering sun and catch
The reddening light of its eclipse
And break it in their tips.

The wood's partitioned still by walls:
It used to be six fields. Old skulls
Of sheep that can no more or else
Don't care to penetrate the trees
Are placed like ivories.

A mushroom casts a shadow now
On pasture where grey thistles grow
That is as long as they. A ewe
Profiles the light, as singular
As the first and bleakest star.

Day dwindles. And then again
That sound, exultant and unclean:
Something that utterly alone
Drags from the foul air in its throat
A bestial strangled note.

Our ears are tuned now for the third
Rehearsal of that cry, agreed
It was no wonder he was scared
By darkness that grew up with him,
Survival's synonym.

If beast, not less for being unknown
And its feared features never seen,
What comfort could there be from one
Glimpse of its tormented flank,
Jaw dropped, point-blank?

For as we more than willingly
Turn from the tied gate, we know
That there will always be some cry
To break our cherished self-esteem
And every civil dream.

And now we're listening inside
The world that is our living head
For what the worst is that the wood
Hoards to remind us of the night,
That failure of the light.

The hand that reaches to the switch
Is not restrained, and nothing much
Inhibits casual questions which
Put up the falling gate again,
Put off the cry of pain.

Branches for ever meet across
The paths where once was grass
And we revisit less and less,
When all the space is overhead,
Those spaces where they led.

And all the sky holds all the light
That ever was and we must wait
Until it fills again with what,
As valid as a watermark,
Illuminates our dark.

And the sun that hissed into the sea
Flares briefly on us for our share
Of days and casts its shadows to
And fro across the nibbled fields.
And the darkness yields.

A Sudden Hail

Once again it is up and over
The stone stairs, parabola
Of ascent for its own sake.

Such climbing is a kind of entry,
Keeping at a distance like
A courtly petitioning.

Laboured breathing is the guilt of a
Restless creature captured by
The supremely immobile.

The head is lowered and eyes are raised
In deference to altitude
At its purest, crest on crest.

At the top the sky starts to open
Like the drawing of curtains,
Fine veils, a theatre scrim.

And an attic hail sprinkles on moss
A careless largesse, cloud stuff,
The hand of the jeweller.

Up and over: the giant presence
Of what, when we are conscious
Of it, becomes endurance,

Something to be lasted that is there
Still when we find it will not
Last, and looms behind us like

The cruel deliberate legends
Of a mountain race for whom
The sky really is a god

And whose future falls like the seasons
On a receptive landscape,
Short shadows, too soon cut down.

We know it is scattered at random.
We know it is our brief gift
Like the snow's lifted waters,

Like the hail's rough milky diamond
Resting a moment against
The tiny feathers of moss.

After that it is all a downward
Tread, tread on tread, the loud heart
Lifted frankly like a face

That attends to its ordinary
Business in a warm valley,
Living cries, level dealing,

And for whom weather is common talk
With other faces and is
That delight faces can bring.

Lines for a 21st Birthday

The odd year, like interest
Accumulating slowly,
Adds its decisive value.

How can you celebrate it
For whom, for two-thirds of it,
Guineas were no fee or bet?

A score and a year will not
So easily multiply
Into full three score and ten.

But if years were guarantees
Of that distinctive wisdom,
This praise of yours would founder

And Rosalind be fooled by
Touchstone's prattling, Eva by
Sachs's self-important song.

You with clasped palms and a skip
Will soon be departed to
Whatever your prayers pose

But the future is not here
And wherever age drags you
Will always stay out of sight.

It is the happy Kingdom
Of Ago to which you will
Almost certainly return:

The student city with its
Afternoon breakfasts and slept
Deadlines and parked suitcases

And the whole population
Taking in seven-league stride
This dated majority!

To me, though, it is a real
Achievement, a mystery
Of significant numbers.

Think of the pontoon kitchen
On a Gwynedd mountainside
Falling apart: three sevens!

So think, maybe, of these lines
Which like most art do little
But refer back to themselves.

The poem finishes like
Life itself: before you can count
It it is almost over.

Rook Blitz

Once like Crécy tents they pegged the field of battle,
    Cover for prudent or cowardly monarchs,
Setting their long sights down half-obstructed files,
    Biding their time, or gladly exchanged.

But now they have met and agreed on their supremacy.
    Now they patrol their grids at speed.
They control rank upon rank mercilessly,
    Advancing alternately like musketeers.

Being trapped by them is terminal and absolute.
    They steal spellbound pawns like doorknobs.
Their only weakness is at their corners, yet they are perfect
    Turrets, and no one gets in. Or out.

Furies

I see you in your short stride
Aloft in deaf weathers
By sheep-path, ghost-ghylls
And the sufficient berry.

Dreaming a distance above
The light tread of your age,
You walk in a charming shadow
Those dreams unwittingly cast.

Alone on your mountain
With the trickling voice of water,
Listen to the maligned Percy,
Damp on his marble page:

'The poet's self-centred seclusion
Was avenged by the furies
Of an irresistible passion
Pursuing him to speedy ruin.'

What better reason, then,
As the mist comes down,
For a considered descent
Into the visible world?

And to claim stability,
The best and surest virtue
For some peace and survival,
Earth-haunting, impartial.

But don't think you are ever safe
From those attendant furies
Who never seem to obey
The beautiful commands of dreams.

For the commands are theirs
And the power is theirs within them,
And every beauty is theirs
And is all your beauty.

For the veil is rent in those dreams
And we without changing are changed,
Pacing a staggered planet,
Powerless, uneasy, awake.

Past

The wind is never freer
From having hair to blow
When we have left the mountain
Before the early snow.

The grass can grow no taller
Beneath our absent tread
And flowers are never wasted
When all the flowers are dead.

The night comes as it has to.
The moon and Wilbur kiss.
With no one there to see it,
What memories will we miss?

The seasons have no hunger
To please us with their sport,
And only words as restless
Betray what we have thought.

And even those emotions,
From being once exposed,
Are like the closing chapters
Of books forever closed.

Goodbye

One by one they say goodbye.
The plans and promises, like sky,
Are for the moment perfectly clear,
But wait till tomorrow:

A little cloud no bigger than
The parting handshake of a man
Who promises he will be back
Thins on the zenith

And there above the roofscape drift
The gloomy greys that never lift
On friends who calculate their hope
In single figures.

Their lips meet like equations of
Elaborate formulae of love
Which founder on some trivial error
And won't come right.

And so they draw away, unequal.
A gradual goodbye's the sequel
Of yet another episode
That came to nothing.

You are the one who's left behind
And tell yourself you must not mind.
You are the hub of all dispersals
But where does it leave you?

Goodbyes like particles define
Their centre with a random line
That only points back to a past
Hypothesised.

And that event becomes your whole
Existence. It is like a role
That keeps you waiting in the wings
For something to happen.

The play itself, although you wrote it,
Would need another life to float it.
The dialogue is dust, the curtain
Not rising or falling.

Yes, these are the goodbye years,
As though the second of three cheers
Has caught the guests with glasses raised
But horribly empty.

The smiles are fixed upon their faces,
The printed names in all the places,
Someone hands flowers, the cameras flash,
But no one is looking.

You've got just one more red to pot.
You've got to make that crucial shot.
You move up to the table, ready
To take all the colours

And when you see the ivory fall,
A futile trickle of your ball
Leaves you tucked in behind the black,
Lost to the yellow.

As, high and dry on narrowing land
You look about your spit of sand
To see who cares to take the odds
And share it with you,

And what you find is rising tide,
The sun gone down, nowhere to hide
And birds that gather in the air,
Dismally calling.

Yes, this is the time that kills.
The losing shot. The empty skills.
And the wild sense of saying so,
Over and over.

England

Falling towards the map is a controlled illusion,
The text scrolled to the cursor. It is England down there,
Tilted like a display. It is a living space
    Screened for observation,
A gravity-haunted logo, a significant shape
    From which there is no escape.

The shires are whitened with snow, old ploughing
Turned to Aztec friezes and museum crochet.
Between the rafters of weather and the granite flags
    Is a simulated surface
Of plot and portion that we only ever know
    As landscape from below.

It implicates our wish to be welcomed, our resolve
To enter the dull story and to make it remarkable,
To order the memory like a WAAF croupier
    Pushing her heroes across
Inches that are clouds and tiny villages recalling
    Our fear of falling.

At the heart of England we are pursuer and pursued,
Where frozen footprints are the history of that hunt
And towns we think we never visited are like
    Both past and future,
Tremendously distinguished in the willed notation
    Of our imagination.

At the heart of England the drivers are silently crawling
Bumper to bumper, the exits sealed off, the route
A duty to some present but long-forgotten intention
    And the lights are flashing
As if to warn us to keep to the dogged pace
    Of a wry acquisitive race.

At the heart of England we listen to old stories
With an amusement that guarantees their lack of any
   power
To direct our attention to what they may be saying
   And off we stolidly stump
Past the gingerbread cathedral and the factory blur
   To the scenery we prefer.

There the eye is of course directed upwards
As paths respect the mossy boulders and outcrop
Of the heights that induce their steady winding and
   climbing
   Until some point is reached
Where we see the heartland sprawled as in a lap,
   Half-asleep, half-map.

For the most part they are nibbled humps or great ledges
Swathed in rolling mist like experimental theatre:
It suits us to shade the eyes, to stare for coasts.
   From that isolation
On either side adventurous streams agree
   To part and find the sea.

We never join them. They are unjoinable.
And there is nothing much in the end to be done
Except to return either the way we came
   Or to find some other route,
Which with a monument or some woody confusion
   Maintains the illusion.

And time itself is like this, an elder dimension
Whose fondness for a particular country may turn
At a stroke to a sly or bullying disregard,
   Who knows that place is never
The involving predicate that something meant,
   Simply an accident.

And is after all where we truly belong,
Its present moments less comfortable than sofas
And the presences scattered on tables before them
    That say: 'We are England.
This memory. This book. This headline. And all the things
    That such belonging brings.'

As the very first move is the very first mistake,
Even the king's pawn, the dry kiss, the sinister
Lunge of the baby's toes like Johnson leaving
    The room when all has been said,
As what we are today depends on what we have been
    And all that we have seen,

As the bell while it rings has not ceased to summon us
Though we lose count of the strokes, as one match
Added to the whole becomes the Tower of London
    And we come to the end of the chapter,
As what we are today depends on what we are up to
    And all that we try to do,

As fingers reach where fruit must be before they know
The fruit is there, as the deafening tapes babble of love
And mothers not long out of childhood stitch shrouds
    At the cradle, as our star
Will give us short grace when it finally disappears
    And we know the prediction of tears,

As we find ourselves again in places that made us happy
And like bar-haunting actors on tour forget our cues,
As we rise in drowning with Greek cries of discovery,
    As we scribble our lucky numbers
And believe the oracle so that the hair lifts from our head
    As we shiver down in bed,

As time itself is unable to build its little Durham
Against anointed oblivion, and we are acknowledged
Its fool servitors, bearing enormous covered dishes
   Into the hungry hall
Where we overhear the talk, seditious, immensely grand
   That we hardly understand,

So we are left at last with only the hopeless instant,
The newborn innocent or wandering dressing-gowned
   victim
For whom the past must be a fable or abandoned
   Like an exhausted quarry,
For whom the future is that breath beyond the breath
   Taken at the moment of death,

So we are left in the thick of all our extended pleasures,
Hearing in the distance the popping guns moving over
England, and saying quietly, one to another:
   'Something is running for cover,
Something has nowhere to hide out there and likely as not
   Something is being shot,

'Such as the refined but shabby fox, left to die
As a gangster dies, arguing with balletic rhetoric
That when in the paleness of dawn the certainty of pain
   Is fully recognised
There will be no reasoning with it, no arguing at all,
   And we shall lie where we fall.'

The Grey and the Green

'Natural objects are *what we were*.
They are what *we should again
become*. We were nature just as they,
and our culture, by means of reason
and freedom, should lead us back to
nature.'   SCHILLER

I'm writing lazily upon
A day in late July, from Wales,
With nettles standing by the wall,
Grasses uncomfortably tall,
And in the grasses, snails.

With such abundance I shall need
No theme, the theme is all about me:
The evidence in stone and oak
Of rampant nature's only joke —
That she can do without me.

However riveting her glance,
I turn my back for half a year
And flowers are standing from the slates,
Spiders are spinning like the fates
And funguses appear:

Wet lips and frills upon the plaster
Like fairies kissing through the ceiling
Show how the rain induced the roof
To cease from standing so aloof
And to respond with feeling.

Rain! It's always up there, busy.
Sometimes it patters like a mouse
Or drums in boredom on the pane.
It stops, and starts, then stops again
And eavesdrops round the house.

It drifts in clouds against the mountain,
Swells the streams and starts to pour
In torrents down the slopes behind
The house and in the house, to find
Its way out through the door.

Sometimes it thunders on the skylights
As though being poured out by a jug.
This brief but mesmerising rain's
Succeeded by the helpless drain's
Protracted glug-glug-glug.

The gutters weep whole afternoons.
The contents of the sky, displayed
In sheets across the fields, aim at
The grass as if to beat it flat,
A drop for every blade.

Within our fenced and sheepless plot
The grasses work their grassy wills.
Rye and timothy and dock,
They cluster at the step and knock
Against the window sills.

Natural things are what we were
And what we should become again.
Once we were nature as they are,
And lug about beneath our star
The matter we were then.

So should our culture (said the Romantic
German in that sowing season
Of the soul's freedom) rightly take us
Back to our paradisal acres
Through liberty and reason.

You can be sure I feel the pull
Of all nostalgic mythic Edens,
But oh, how very hard it is
To see that arguments like his
Lend their design much credence.

For liberty in our sense never
Kept house with nature in the raw.
I think of Milton (as I scythe
The tangled clumps of green that writhe
In freedom at our door)

Whose message was that temperance
Requires the energy it curbs,
As syntax shaping sentences
Is happier not with simply 'is'
But much more active verbs;

That civil order shows the fairer
When mastering the pulse of riot;
That good is known by evil, just
As love springs from the cease of lust,
From fretful chaos, quiet.

The rage of the homunculus
To nuzzle in the blinding yolk
Requires an absolute devotion
We must deny, and no emotion
Insists that we must choke.

So my firm mowing arm controls
A green and sprouting commonweal.
The populations of the field,
Clock and seed and fruitage, yield
To government of steel.

Down falls the crested hair-grass, reed
Canary, oat; the barley's comb
And timothy's thick tail; the tender
Tree-palace of the bent; the slender
Fox-tail and the brome.

Where something like a nursery stood
Of lecherous grasses yet unborn,
See now their ravings quieten to
A neutered peace I can sit through,
A deckchair on a lawn.

Where on my knee a book can rest,
Where on the page my hand can think,
Where in my hand the Edding edds
Through which the mind in humour weds
Passionless thought and ink.

The mind, it may be said, and what
Is that? The mind is grass, alas!
It's all or nothing, that's the trouble
(I ponder on that velvet stubble,
Pouring another glass).

It's either everything we must
Become, or it's a giant con.
It's something we're amazed at, some
Impulsion — or it's like a bum,
Something to fall upon.

Who would not rather be a mindless
Grass? Locked in that quilted field,
No need to feel that it's of use,
Pollen and root and primal juice
In a green tube concealed.

With no pretence at calculation,
Hope or fear or memory,
Its head reveals its simple needs
In tapered symmetry of seeds
Tip-toeing to be free.

Our heads have long ago exchanged
The simple green for black and white.
Our good is lost, we do not need it.
Or if we think we do, we read it —
If someone else can write.

From noisy theatres of life
Our heads are full of long retreats
Where self-appointed NCOs
Exhort us daily in foul prose
From even fouler sheets.

Sunday mornings are devoted
To the required responses, civil
Arguments and qualifications;
To self-sufficient explanations
And other sorts of drivel.

The paragraphs of prescience,
The columns on calamity,
Are always just a little late
And, though so true, congratulate
Their authors with a fee.

And what is written may be thought,
Suffered or performed somewhere.
We're told it is, but then the telling
Becomes the product it is selling:
How can we ever care?

In solipsistic boogie-packs
Of cultural bandage we skate deaf
Through tower-blocks of necessity,
Protected from their shouting by,
For instance, Brahms in F.

Such music tries to tell us that
The air is yearning to contain
Whatever consonance of passion
Happens to be the current fashion
Of disembodied pain.

Culture creates élites of failure
And heroes of those tortured wrecks
Who at its prompting are most prompt
To issue chaste denials, swamped
By the hopelessness of sex.

The adolescent grass is not
Ashamed, is never seen to blush.
No secret hankering occurs,
Nor each *amitié amoureuse*
Turns to a helpless crush.

It does not calculate or risk.
Pleasure's unknown and so is force.
It does not crawl across the bed
And is too steadfast and well-bred
To contemplate divorce.

Nor does it regulate in verse
Complete disruptions of its soul.
No sublimation of *tendresse*
Promotes an urgency to bless
Another's vital role.

For one grass of a certain kind
Is not much different from another.
Its blind asexual reproduction
Requires no tea-time introduction,
Has never heard of mother.

It's not quite envy that we feel:
The sturdiness, the ignorance,
The generosity, the stillness,
Show love as an absorbing illness
That makes a choice of chance.

And in that paradox we live
As in the aura of a crime
That we regret but made us rich,
Too conscious of a truth for which
There's always or never time.

Living a good way up a mountain
Above the natural line of trees,
We nurture saplings, ache for torn
Or wounded cedar, oak or thorn
And mourn fatalities.

Trees are annual calendars
And their expressive flags have taught us
To greet the spring. They're twiggy babels
For many birds; pencils and tables
To please our daughters' daughters.

The lifetime that they take to grow
Is rarely ours. We feel a bond
Like that with age: memorabilia
To be respected, grave, familiar,
A little feared or fond.

We note the fruiting of the rowan,
If it's the year for bullace or
For sloe, or how much higher stand
The valiant Blackheath walnut and
The Oxford sycamore.

But most regret in this last winter
The passing of an ancient ash
Which air, that changed location at
Unlikely speed, disturbed and flat-
tened with an unheard crash.

But now, although it leans upon
One hinge of bark, new leafage shoots
From stumps the guilty wind has healed.
It dipped its elbows in the field
And there established roots.

If only our unrooted lives
When felled could simply change direction
And all our tall assumptions both
Be trimmed and find amazing growth,
A perfect resurrection!

The tree has found a way of walking
Not as our childhood stories told us
Through sudden supernatural strength
But through first tumbling its full length
Then growing from its shoulders.

A saint might get to Bardsey by
A slow deliberate prostration,
And such a gradual pilgrimage
Would postulate at every stage
A halting in his station.

And we could take our time like this
Were life as long as it is wide,
With no regretful glances back
At all the branchings of the track,
A lifetime for one stride.

I have a notion, though, that even
So we could not much rejoice
At what we'd done or where we'd got to:
What *is* requires to know what's *not*, to
Exercise its choice.

Perhaps we need alternatives.
Perhaps we need to make mistakes.
The will unfortunately thrives
On possibility: our lives
Must rise — or sink, like cakes.

And now the bees are sawing flowers,
As casual in the endeavour
As if the petals on each stem
Had fallen open just for them
And the sun would last for ever.

And other creatures in the grass
Move in their leggy purposes:
A caterpillar scurries hard
Across the warm particular yard
Of hillside that is his.

A beetle, tilted in the green,
Gropes with his antlers for a purchase,
And even from my chair I see
Its blackness inching to be free
In tiny wavering lurches.

Down there are even lesser beings
Who do not have the need to walk,
Nothing to make them climb or stretch,
Nothing to carry, nothing to fetch:
They simply hug a stalk.

You'd need a microscopic eye
To see them blind and massed and thronging.
Although their grassy life seems bleak
It is a vertical, unique
Achievement of belonging.

Few other sounds: the distant snigger
Of buzzards; the complaining tones
Of sheep; the crumpling of the small
Stream as it makes its shallow fall
Over the worn stones.

And always the sun arcing above
The fret that creeps below us still
Like a brave hand that quietly clears
The sky of its forgotten tears
And sends them down the hill.

It times itself across the mountains:
Tre'r Ceiri's nine o'clock, at three
The middle mountain, dusk the quarry.
It hangs upon the promontory
And sinks into the sea.

It's no surprise to find the sun
Intoxicating: we drink deep,
A summer's depth, a draught imbued
With every idle summer mood
Of love or wit or sleep.

Imperious season! It calls us up
In our unusual calm and fitness
Willingly to mount the stand
And take our future by the hand
In unreliable witness.

As though we just might go on living,
Our testimony never waver
And our condition be the same,
Always to have a right to claim
That judgement in our favour.

But summers come and summers go,
A flourish on the signature
Of the year's cheques, and we the claimant
Of punctual everlasting payment
Have no right to be sure.

A voice is calling down the field,
A trick of the light, or in the ear
The slightest shift, a distant saw,
A sudden rapping on the door,
Brings that familiar fear.

As harvest bends beneath the wind
Or trees are stirred or grasses bowed
When it disturbs the valley's surface
From the chilled wood to where the turf is
Darkened by a cloud.

Until the darkness that our lives
Will unavoidably arrange,
We have this pact to keep in peace
Our favoured landscape till time cease
To hesitate from change.

And Never is a world away
From Now, as Other is from Me.
The solipsist can hardly find
That time weighs heavy on his mind,
Self is eternity.

As on the mountain starry moss
Lies open to the sky unseen:
Proliferating radials are
A perfect mockery of star,
Pale on the darker green.

And yet those systems so like eyes
Are wholly inward, slow to change:
No observation, no reflection,
No intercourse and no connection,
Sightless, profuse and strange.

Is mind to be compared with these?
An accidental peal of bells?
Astronomy's congratulation?
Random organic integration,
A colony of cells?

You will not find the elusive mind
By cutting up a living brain.
As well might fronds of wire be seen
To sprout up from a grey machine
Or grasses rust in rain.

Our new computer in the eaves
Copes with the problems we have set it.
It finds square roots, defines an arc,
Plays asteroids or J. S. Bach
Or anything we let it.

Between the keyboard and the screen
Lies hidden electronic finery
That turns what either of you says
Into electric impulses.
Its simple code is binary.

It makes with anyone who chooses
Its Mephistophelean bargain
To help you to achieve your goal
Provided that you lose your soul
And use the proper jargon.

But I am not with those who fear
Such speed and rational procedure,
For as a model of the brain
It's much superior, it is plain,
To such things as Ouija.

The only problem is, the thing
Is motiveless, immortal, neuter,
You look for something like a mind
In vain, for all you'll ever find
Inside is a computer.

And what it does is limited
To what its program makes it do.
The power of the computer buff
Can only prove, alas, enough
To see his program through.

And that elusive element
Beyond determination still
Eludes. No god could tolerate
A being that he must create
In bonds, without free will.

A tool then, not a creature which
Is appetitive though obedient
Through recognition of its good:
It lacks that one misunderstood
Mysterious ingredient.

What do we call it? Nature? Life?
Where do we find it? Beyond the stammer
Of electronics freely move
Millions of nouns that seem to prove
An independent grammar.

Beyond the slavish rigmarole
Of subroutine and variable,
The soft world's at its nightly ruses.
The tiniest midge still somehow chooses
To find itself in trouble.

When all the sun there is touches
The sea, and grey invests the green,
Eater and eaten flitter by,
A demonstration to defy
The passionless machine.

Horny and muffled moths whir through
The window, summoned by its glow,
And in the park of its display
Quizzing each Goto and array
Stroll stiffly to and fro.

The moon itself, the light they think
It is, is no less readable.
Its hieroglyphics are the history
Of an unfathomable mystery,
The grave celestial pull.

What wonder that the dandy moth,
Preening itself in its fur collar
And muttering in its whiskery muzzle,
Ignores the lesser luminous puzzle
Of waiting Inkey$?

So it might wait for ever if
No one could see its flashing cursor,
In a vast emptiness, unfree,
Deserted by humanity
(Or perhaps vice versa).

For if a desert is in question,
It's possible machines will make it.
The world, which has not lasted long
And may not, is going for a song
And no one wants to take it.

Should we bequeath it to the moth?
It needs some strange nocturnal creature
Like the gowned bat that haunts the house,
A crucified aerial mouse,
A tiny baleful preacher.

A world of bats and cold machines!
I do not find the thought endearing.
Programs survive though current fails,
Inscrutable as the bat's wails,
Voices unheard, unhearing.

The universe is full of noises
And rather fewer ears. The gift
Of sight is rare enough for stars
To die unseen. We can touch Mars
But galaxies go unsniffed.

It is our aim to use our senses
Rightly, senses of every sort.
Computers are a harnessed force,
No revolution; they endorse
Traditional ways of thought.

It's hard, though, not to feel that when
I play a game of chess with one
It has a personality.
It gives a bleep to welcome me
Whenever I switch on.

Two pairs of OOs move up and down
As though, while pondering, it scanned
Visible possibilities.
God knows, though, what it really 'sees'.
Nothing that's not been planned.

Those tell-tale traits I find attractive
Mean all that its instructions mean.
Its program tells it what to do.
Nothing it does is really new
Or entirely unforeseen.

It doesn't joke. It plays five games
Straight off and doesn't mind five more.
It won't admit a move is clever
Or make illegal moves. It never
Offers me a draw.

It doesn't like a glass of something,
Ignores all flattery, loves to play
The French Defence and risks its neck
Through ignorance of discovered check
More than a move away.

Losing the endgame makes it most
Like a person, least inert:
It gives up the defence, plays wild,
Moves distant pieces, like a child,
Hopeless, defeatist, hurt.

And such, perhaps, we really are
If mind is only an illusion,
A more or less determined process,
Part of itself, a true hypnosis,
A triumph of confusion.

Arraigned in our material being
The sentence of the court is binding:
Mind is the evidence we show
Of knowing that we do not know,
Of minding, and not minding.

It is the evidence and judgement, too:
Our mindfulness reminds us of it
At all those times when ignorance
Of what we call our loss, by chance,
Might turn it to our profit.

Fatal cognisance! As though
A frown in the flower means it fears
The absence of the bee — instead
Of some decision to be red
Until the bee appears.

Or yellow, plain, fantastical,
Long-lived or short, but never knowing
The pride of colour or the term
Of life, nothing beyond the firm
Root and grip of growing.

For flowers, mind is only touch.
Green is the colour that began it,
Green the sign of the cell's toil,
A touch of sky, a touch of soil,
The ladder of the planet.

Green is the negative of stars,
Green is the mirror of the sun,
Green is the cooling of earth's fire:
A height from which we have reached higher,
But the best thing earth has done.

A daily hunger tells us we
Are planet, too. That is our root,
Ingesting green. Our meals should prove
We have a root at a remove,
A liberated root.

The body is not user-friendly
(Examples of it we have hugged
Show that its program, though involved,
Still has procedures to be solved,
Commands to be debugged).

Perhaps too liberated, then,
A simple hunger turned to greed?
Imperious inorganic lives
Inform us that mere being thrives
Without that cycled need.

Enchanted earth already turned
To stone, the mountain feels no lack
Of purpose when it is demolished:
Granite is patient still unpolished,
The grey that turns to black.

Grey still undynamited, grey
In crumbled boulders, grey half-grey
Half-ground to that swart glassiness
That graced the dead's last known address
When their souls had flown away.

In amphitheatres of absence
All the machinery is rust.
Slabs, kerbs and banks' façades,
Half-turned curling stones and shards,
Loose gravel, grit and dust

Remain like broken toys to show
What men destroyed a mountain for,
What sudden hunger or excuse
Used it, and left it after use
Half-eaten to the core.

And on the hillside older stones
Make other spaces out of grey:
Windows and doors are holes that show
The light that it may come and go,
A man that he may stay.

The walls are plastered white inside
To veil the stone from scrutiny:
As to a squared-off globe all four
Meet the horizon of the floor
Like a descending sky.

Tiles mimic earth, and rafters boughs,
Curtains are clouds against the sun.
Roomscapes to be conventional
Require a foreground: pastoral
Upholstery for one.

Quarryman and farmer lay
Their arms along its arms and doze.
Its back confers upon the skills
And elbows that explored the hills
Its purpose of repose.

A chair affords its occupant
A sense of being offered to
Some present prospect of content
As though a god, forgiving, sent
A slumber or a view.

As though its seat, through being
Raised from earth, diminished its
Compelling gravity, conferred
On its incumbent, like a bird,
A freedom where he sits

And takes his ease after some pleasing
Labour, motionless, coeval
With the hills in everything
But age, taking their shape, taking
Their air of past upheaval

That lends a present dignity
To their resigned deliberate
Collapse, as if outlasting what
They have outlasted brought them not
Too early or too late

Into their own identity;
When grey retirement's turned-down page
Looks back upon a hero who
Has long desired to pass into
An unperturbed old age.

A mountain is a mountain is
Itself, lasting, indifferent, proud.
The poet on his human throne
Has often wished that he were stone,
Or fluid, or a cloud.

Grasping the palpable, he feels
All that is vagrant in him lift
At the touch. A single fragile link
Offers an anchor he can sink
Into the friendless drift.

And now even the thought of these
Completed peaks, purpled above
Their green and still-grazed shoulders, brings
The shaping calm of well-loved things
Outside our human love

Whose blessing is unspoken like
An institution's is to those
Who freely seek in its employment
Their chaste hopes and loyal enjoyment
So that it never goes

But stands for all time in the shape
Of what it is and has been, till
Its fond dismissal sets us free
From it, and life, and all that we
Might be and never will.

So in the shade of the three mountains
I sit from day to day and teach
The inward eye its signs: from ledge
And scree they run, from slope and hedge
Down to Will Parsal's beach.

Mushrooms put tents up in the field
Where lofted thistles sail and spill.
Three horses come for sugar, late
Against the sun, and by the gate
The lane leads down the hill.

We are at peace here, where the grass
Extends however far we roam
And we can be, without having crossed
A road, tired out and almost lost
In a wood, but nearly home.

It is the world, and so it should be.
And it is ever so, once seen.
For the mind has caught it in its season
And there it is, and for no reason:
The grey among the green.